CRYPTID GUIDES: CREATURES OF FOLKLORE

GUIDE TO MUMMIES

A Crabtree Branches Book

BY CARRIE GLEASON

Crabtree Publishing
crabtreebooks.com

Developed and produced by Plan B Book Packagers
www.planbbookpackagers.com
Art director: Rosie Gowsell Pattison

Crabtree editor: Ellen Rodger
Prepress technician: Margaret Salter
Production coordinator: Katherine Berti
Proofreader: Melissa Boyce

Photographs:
Pg 8 Rosie Gowsell; pg 29 Huangdan2060-Wikipedia;
all other images Shutterstock.com.

Crabtree Publishing

crabtreebooks.com   800-387-7650

Hardcover   978-1-0396-6344-2
Paperback   978-1-0396-6393-0
Ebook (pdf)   978-1-0398-0719-8
Epub   978-1-0398-0746-4

Published in Canada
Crabtree Publishing
616 Welland Avenue
St. Catharines, Ontario
L2M 5V6

Published in the United States
Crabtree Publishing
347 Fifth Avenue
Suite 1402-145
New York, NY 10016

Library and Archives Canada
Cataloguing in Publication
Available at Library and Archives Canada

Library of Congress
Cataloging-in-Publication Data
Available at the Library of Congress

Printed in the U.S.A./012023/CG20220815

CONTENTS

CRYPTIDS and KINFOLK

This chart shows some of the best-known cryptids and creatures from folklore. How many of them do you think are real?

LAND DWELLER

UNDEAD

LIVING

SPIRIT

LIVING CORPSE

HUMANOID

Ghost

Zombie

Mummy

Werewolf

Werecat

Banshee

Grim Reaper

Ghoul

Vampire

Bigfoot

Mothman

Yeti

Yeren

Yowie

WHAT IS A MUMMY?

Mummies are real. Monster mummies that seem to be alive, however, are creatures from folklore. Folklore is filled with many different types of creatures that are generally believed to be made up, such as werewolves, zombies, and giants. Other creatures from folklore are cryptids, which are animals that may or may not exist, such as the Loch Ness Monster. The information about mummies in this book comes from legends about mummies. Could monster mummies be real? This Cryptid Guide will help you decide!

ANIMAL & HYBRID

Unicorn

Jackalope

Chupacabra

OTHERWORLDLY

Fairy

Elf

Nymph

GIANT

Ogre

Troll

SEA MONSTER

EXTRATERRESTRIAL

Alien

SWAMP MONSTER

Mermaid

Sea Serpent

LAKE MONSTER

Louisiana Swamp Monster

Leviathan

Loch Ness Monster

Ogopogo

Champ

5

FEAR THE MUMMY...

Imagine this: It's long, long ago and you're hanging around a dock in Egypt, watching men load large wooden crates onto a ship. A man with pale skin calls you over and says he'll pay you to help them load the boat. You agree, but as you lift one of the crates, the lid slips off and you see what's inside—the golden death mask of an ancient ruler called a pharaoh. A chill runs down your spine. Inside that crate is a mummy, and the rumor is that disturbing the burial sites of the pharaohs means trouble. You need to get away from there—fast! As you hurry to leave the site, you trip and fall over a rock, twisting your ankle. Then, suddenly, you see a cloud of flying insects coming your way. Thunder booms, lightning rips across the sky, and rain starts to pour down on you. There's only one explanation for your sudden bad luck—a mummy's curse!

MUMMY BASICS

Most mummies are very old dead bodies that have been preserved. Some, such as the ones found in ancient Egyptian tombs, were created on purpose. Others were created when dead bodies were exposed to extreme cold, dryness, or other natural conditions. Mummy legends and folklore tell of powerful curses that can bring misfortune to people who disturb the tombs of mummies, or even bring them back to life! These kinds of stories have appeared in books and movies and have led to the creation of the monster mummies we know—and love—today.

THE UNDEAD

Vampires

Vampires come from Eastern European folklore. They are said to have once been living, breathing people who have risen from the dead, and must drink blood to survive.

Zombies

Zombies come from the folklore of Haiti, a Caribbean country. Haitian zombies are people who have been cursed and enslaved by a powerful witch. Zombies in popular culture today are undead creatures that have been infected by a virus and eat human brains.

Ghouls

In Arabian folklore, ghouls are shapeshifting demons or spirits that live in graveyards or deserts. Modern ghouls are said to eat human flesh.

ANATOMY OF A MUMMY

Monster mummies—they're dusty and disheveled, moaning and groaning, trailing their wrappings behind them. Here's how to spot a mummy.

Not very smart, as their brains have likely been removed

May still have teeth, although they have cavities due to lack of dental care in ancient times

Usually quite thin, because their internal organs may have been removed

May smell like perfume or spices

Skin and flesh may either be preserved under the wrappings or have been stripped away and replaced by clay

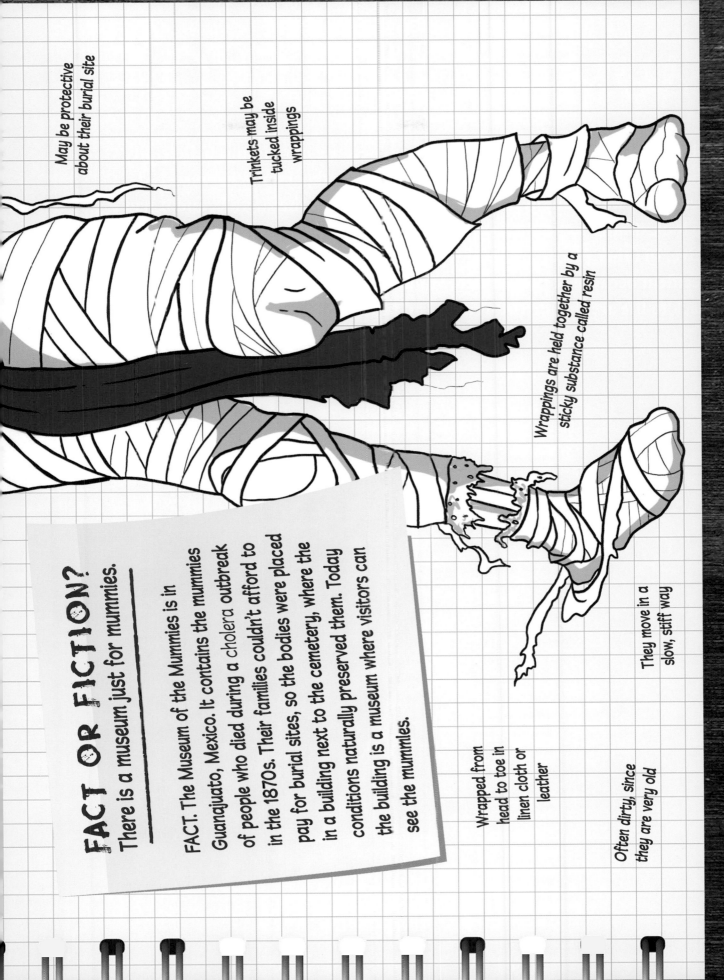

May be protective about their burial site

Trinkets may be tucked inside wrappings

Wrappings are held together by a sticky substance called resin

FACT OR FICTION?
There is a museum just for mummies.

FACT. The Museum of the Mummies is in Guanajuato, Mexico. It contains the mummies of people who died during a cholera outbreak in the 1870s. Their families couldn't afford to pay for burial sites, so the bodies were placed in a building next to the cemetery, where the conditions naturally preserved them. Today the building is a museum where visitors can see the mummies.

Wrapped from head to toe in linen cloth or leather

Often dirty, since they are very old

They move in a slow, stiff way

MUMMY LIFE CYCLE

Mummies were created in ancient times because of religious beliefs. In the religion of ancient Egypt, the body of a dead person was preserved because it was thought that they would need it in the afterlife, and it had to look similar to how it looked when the person was alive. In other places, mummies were created by accident because of the climate. Mummies that come back to life are the idea of writers and filmmakers.

A body starts to rot just 24 hours after death. If you have ever been to a funeral and seen a body in a casket, that body has also been preserved in some way, although not enough to make it a mummy. It was also likely wearing makeup—to make it look less dead!

STAGE 1: DEATH

Who gets to be a mummy?

- If you were a ruler or important person in ancient Egypt, you might be very carefully mummified and placed in a sealed tomb with all kinds of treasures. Ordinary people were mummified too, but in a much less fancy way.

- If you were a child in the ancient Inca civilization, you might become a mummy if you were offered as a sacrifice to the gods. These mummies were drugged before death and left to die on mountain tops.

STAGE 2: MUMMIFICATION

Dead bodies naturally decompose, or rot, over time. This is caused by tiny living things called bacteria that break down the body. To mummify a body, steps need to be taken to prevent it from rotting, such as:

- Hiring an embalmer. A skilled worker called an embalmer can stop a body from rotting. An embalmer cleans a body, uses substances to preserve it, and then makes it look similar to how it looked when alive.

- Put it somewhere that bacteria can't grow. Without bacteria, a body will not rot. Bacteria cannot thrive in extreme temperatures or places with little oxygen. Some good places for naturally creating mummies include:

  - a type of swamp called a peat bog, where there is little oxygen
  - the top of a snow- or ice-covered mountain, where it is freezing cold and there is less oxygen in the air
  - a hot, dry desert

STAGE 3: REANIMATION

In folklore and popular culture, stories are told of mummies that are reawakened when their tombs are disturbed. The tombs of kings and queens in ancient Egypt had warnings written on them not to disturb them. These warnings led to the idea that mummies held curses and could cause bad luck or even rise from the dead to protect their tomb.

STAGE 4: DEATH (AGAIN)

In this stage, a mummy returns to death. It might even finally go on to the afterlife.

MUMMIES AROUND THE WORLD

The best-known real mummies are those of pharaohs found in tombs in Egypt. But mummies have been found all over the world. And many are still being discovered today.

1 The Aztec people of Mexico made mummy "bundles." These mummies had their arms and legs tied with rope to hold them in place.

2 The Inca of the Andes Mountains in what is now Peru wrapped mummies in leather or cloth and placed them in large baskets or pottery jars.

3 The Atacama Desert, in what is now Chile, is one of the driest places on Earth. Here, the Chinchorro civilization made mummies by removing the dead person's skin and replacing it with a clay mask. Internal organs were also removed and replaced with vegetable fibers or animal hair. Bodies were wrapped in long, grassy plants and left out to dry.

1 Mexico

2 Peru

3 Chile

4 Egypt

5 Europe

6 China

7 Philippines

8 New Zealand

6

In northwestern China, in an area known as the Tarim Basin, 200 graves containing people who were naturally mummified in the Taklamakan Desert have been found. These mummies have European-style features and red, blonde, or light-brown hair. They were found buried in wooden, boat-shaped coffins, with grave markers sticking out of the sand. Who they were is a mystery.

BEWARE: A FACT!

There are mummies on Mount Everest! The world's tallest mountain is a very cold place and there is less oxygen higher up the mountain. Climbers who died on the journey to the top have been found preserved on the mountain. It is too dangerous to try and bring these bodies back down the mountain.

5

In northwestern Europe, hundreds of ancient dead bodies have been found preserved in peat bogs. The skin of these mummies is stained black or brown from the peat. These "bog bodies" usually died violently and may have been sacrifices to ancient gods.

4

The ancient Egyptians mummified kings and queens and buried them in pyramids and in tombs in the Valley of the Kings and the Valley of the Queens.

8

The Maori, the Indigenous peoples of New Zealand, mummified just the heads of the dead. They removed the eyes and brain and sealed the holes with flax fiber and tree gum. The head was then boiled or steamed in an oven, smoked, and left to dry in the sunlight for several days. Afterward it was rubbed with shark oil and tattooed.

7

People in the northern Philippines made "fire mummies." To make a fire mummy, a person was given a salty mixture to drink before they died. After death, the body was washed and set over a fire in a seated position, where the heat and smoke would dry out the corpse. To dry out the internal organs, smoke was blown into the body. Herbs were rubbed on the body and it was placed in a wooden coffin and laid to rest in a cave.

GUIDES TO THE AFTERLIFE

People throughout time have had different ideas about death and what happens after we die. Many cultures believe in an afterlife, where the souls of the dead go to live forever. Often in a culture's myths and legends, there are gods or other supernatural beings who help the dead reach the afterlife.

HERMES

The ancient Greek god Hermes guided souls to the afterlife, a place called Hades. Hermes could move freely between the worlds of the gods and the living and was described as having winged sandals. Once the dead reached Hades, they were prevented from leaving by a three-headed guard dog named Cerberus.

YAMA

In the myths of ancient India, Yama is the god of death and justice. He is sometimes shown holding a mace and a piece of rope called a noose to catch the souls of sinners. Yama rules over the spirits of dead ancestors in the Hindu religion.

ANUBIS

Anubis is the god of death, embalming, and the protector of tombs in the religion of ancient Egypt. He is often shown as a jackal or as a man with the head of a jackal. Anubis took souls to the afterlife, called Duat, and performed a ceremony in which he weighed their hearts against a "feather of truth" to see if they should be allowed to stay.

VALKYRIES

In Norse mythology, valkyries were female warriors who served the god Odin. They guided the souls of warriors killed in battle to Valhalla. It was a great honor for a warrior to go to Valhalla, which is the grand hall of Odin. There, warriors wait for Ragnarok, a final battle that will mark the end of the world.

XOLOTL

Xolotl guided dead souls to Mictlan, which was the Aztec land of the dead. According to Aztec beliefs, Mictlan had nine levels and it took four years to reach the last level. Along the way, the dead person faced challenges and was accompanied by Xolotl, who is shown in Aztec art as a dog-headed man or a skeleton.

THE GRIM REAPER

Europe in the 1300s was the time of the Black Death—a deadly plague that spread through the land and killed up to one-third of the population. Around this time the idea of the Grim Reaper, a skeleton figure wearing a black cloak and carrying a scythe, came about. A scythe was a tool that farmers used at the time to harvest, or cut down crops for collection. Instead of crops, the Grim Reaper collects, or "reaps," the souls of the dead.

HOW TO MAKE AN EGYPTIAN MUMMY

The key to making a mummy is to find a way to prevent it from rotting. Throughout history, different cultures had their own ways of making mummies. These methods changed over time.

HAPY (BABOON): LUNGS

DUAMUTEF (JACKAL): STOMACH

STORING ORGANS

Ancient Egyptians believed that the dead would need their organs again in the afterlife, so they placed them in jars, called canopic jars, in the tomb. Each of the four jars held a different organ and was protected by its own god, known together as the Four Sons of Horus. Each jar had a lid in the shape of the head of the god responsible for the organ.

IMSETY (HUMAN HEAD): LIVER

EGYPTIAN MUMMY-MAKING 101

STEP 1

Make cuts in the body to remove the internal organs, such as the lungs, liver, stomach, and intestines. The brain can be pulled out through the nostrils using a large hook. Throw away the brain, but keep the other organs and leave them to dry out, as these will be needed in the afterlife. The heart, which is believed to contain a person's soul, can remain in the body.

STEP 2

Clean and rinse the body. Rub it with oil and spices.

STEP 3

Cover the body in a kind of salt called natron, which dries it out. Leave for 40 days.

STEP 4

Stuff the body with linen, feathers, or some other natural fibers to give it shape.

STEP 5

Wrap the body in a type of cloth called linen. If wrapping a pharaoh or other important person, place amulets, which were valuable trinkets believed to aid in the afterlife, between the layers of cloth.

STEP 6

Apply a coat of resin to the mummy to seal it. Resin is a substance that helps make it waterproof.

STEP 7

Place the mummy in a coffin called a sarcophagus, in a tomb with treasures. Some mummies were placed in more than one coffin, one inside the other. The sarcophagus was usually painted and inscribed with the person's name.

QEBEHSENUEF
(FALCON):
INTESTINES

MUMMY VS SKELETON

The difference between a mummy and a skeleton is that a mummy has had some of its organs and soft tissues preserved. A skeleton is just bone—it's what's left after all the soft, moist parts of a body rot. Except in the case of bog bodies, most mummies still have their skeletons intact. For mummies preserved in bogs, the acidity of the bog causes the bones to weaken and decay, while the skin and other soft tissues are perfectly preserved.

MUMMY

A mummy is a dead body that has had some of its skin, organs, or soft tissues preserved. Organs are things such as the heart, liver, and stomach. Soft tissues are body parts that connect or support organs and bones. They include muscles, fat, blood vessels, and tendons.

HUMAN FOSSILS

Fossils, whether animal or human, are rocks. They are not the remains of the creature itself. Fossils form after the soft tissue and organs have rotted away, and after the bone of the skeleton has started to break down. The best place for a fossil to form is on a seabed or riverbed. There, tiny pieces of rocks and minerals called sediment seep through decaying bone, replacing organic matter with minerals. Human fossils are usually much older than mummies and skeletons.

SKELETON

A skeleton is just the bones that are left after all the other body parts, including skin, organs, and soft tissues, have decayed or rotted away. How long it takes for a body to become a pile of bones depends on the temperature, moisture, and oxygen at its burial site. Bones take anywhere from 20 to 1,000 years to decay!

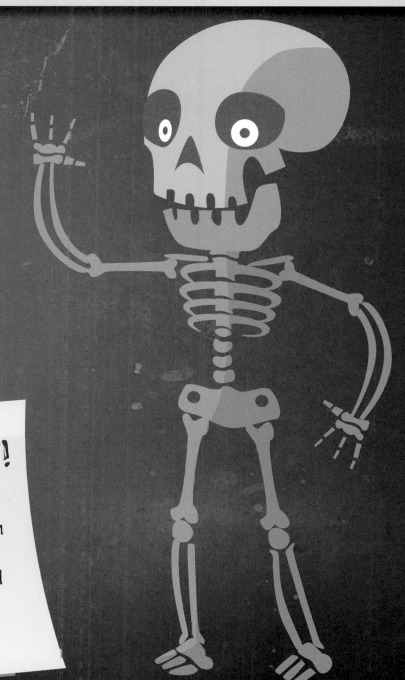

BEWARE: A FACT!

In Peru, the Inca dressed up mummies of important people and brought them to events. They even offered these mummies food and drink, and treated them as though they were alive.

MUMMY MANIA

For thousands of years, the tombs of Egyptian mummies were a treasure trove for grave robbers. The builders of burial tombs took steps to try and keep the treasures safe by adding false doors, secret rooms, and fake walls. But grave robbers from ancient to modern times still found their way in and stole the treasures that people were buried with—they even stole the mummies themselves!

MUMMY POWDER

One of the uses for stolen mummies was to make "mummia" or mummy powder. Mummia was popular in Europe from the 1200s to the 1700s as a medicine to treat wounds, pain, and even coughs. Originally the recipe for mummia called for a natural sticky black substance called bitumen. But over time, people came to believe that it was made from mummies, so ground-up mummies from Egypt were traded to Europe for the medicine.

UNWRAPPING PARTIES

People in Europe in the 1800s were fascinated with ancient Egypt. Travelers to Egypt could buy ancient artifacts from street vendors that had been looted from tombs. Even whole mummies could be purchased and brought home. In Europe, wealthy people hosted "unwrapping parties." People were invited to these parties to dine, drink, dance, and visit, but the highlight of the evening would be the unwrapping of a real-life Egyptian mummy!

Parties where mummies are unwrapped may seem gruesome to us today, but at the time, operations on living people were also sometimes public events. Operations took place in operating theaters where medical students and the public could pay to watch doctors cut someone open or perform autopsies on the dead.

THE MUMMY'S CURSE

The idea that a mummy's tomb is cursed grew popular when the tomb of the Egyptian pharaoh Tutankhamun was discovered in 1922 by British archaeologist Howard Carter. After excavation of the tomb began, people started to mysteriously and unexpectedly die. The idea that these deaths were caused by a curse took hold in newspapers and the rumor of the curse spread around the world. This timeline shows some of the mysterious deaths associated with the curse of King Tut's tomb.

April 1923

Name: George Herbert (aka Lord Carvarvon)

Role: **Paid for the excavation**

Death: **Caused by an infected mosquito bite.**

Other mysterious events at the time of his death include a power outage in Cairo (the city in Egypt where he died), and the death of his dog Susie, at home in England on the same day.

February 1924

Name: **Sir Archibald Reid**

Role: **A radiologist who was asked to X-ray the mummy**

Death: **Failed abdominal surgery in Switzerland (before he could even get to Egypt!)**

Name: Georges Bénédite
Role: A well-known French archaeologist in Egypt

Death: Died from a fall shortly after visiting the site of King Tutankhamun's tomb

Name: Richard Bethell
Role: Howard Carter's assistant and the second person, after Carter, to enter the tomb

Death: Found dead in his bed, a suspected victim of smothering. A year later, Bethell's elderly father, unable to cope with his son's death, died after jumping from a window.

March 1926

November 1929

September 1924

April 1928

Name: Hugh Evelyn-White
Role: British archaeologist who helped excavate the tomb

Death: Hung himself two years after working on the excavation in Egypt. He left a note saying he was cursed.

Name: Arthur Mace
Role: An archaeologist who worked at the site

Death: Became ill with a chest infection while working at the site and was forced to return home to England, where he died a few years later, possibly from poisoning

MUMMIES MAKE IT BIG

Even before King Tut's tomb was big news, writers were creating stories about mummy curses and mummies returning to life. Often in stories about mummy monsters they are looking for revenge for disturbing their tomb.

1959
A new *The Mummy* movie is made, which borrows elements from earlier mummy movies. This time the monster mummy Kharis is brought back to life with the words from an ancient scroll.

1955
The comedy film *Abbott and Costello Meet the Mummy* is released. In the film, two characters dress up as mummies and meet a "real" mummy.

1973
The Marvel comic book character N'Kantu the Living Mummy is created. N'Kantu was mummified by having all of his blood drained and replaced with another substance.

1987
The comedy-horror movie *The Monster Squad* is released. In it, a group of kids tries to stop monsters from folklore—including a mummy—from taking over the world.

2021
In the family movie *Under Wraps*, three kids try to save a mummy named Harold from turning to dust.

2017
Another remake of *The Mummy* is made, this one starring action-adventure actor Tom Cruise.

1827
The Mummy!, by Jane Loudon, is the first story written in English in which mummies are brought back to life. The story is set in the future, in the year 2126.

1892
The short story "Lot No. 249" by Sir Arthur Conan Doyle, the British writer who created Sherlock Holmes, is published. It is the first story in which an awakened mummy is dangerous.

1903
The Jewel of the Seven Stars, a book by Bram Stoker, author of *Dracula*, is published. The story features a mummy's curse and a mummy cat.

1940
In *The Mummy's Hand*, the mummy Kharis is brought back to life with a magic elixir. Three follow-up movies are made: *The Mummy's Tomb*, *The Mummy's Ghost*, and *The Mummy's Curse*.

1932
The Mummy, starring actor Boris Karloff, who also played Frankenstein's monster, is released. Karloff plays Imhotep, a 3,700-year-old mummy.

1993
The Curse of the Mummy's Tomb is published. It is the sixth book in the original best-selling Goosebumps horror novel series for kids.

1999
The Mummy, the first in a trilogy of action-adventure mummy movies, is released. Two more movies, *The Mummy Returns* and *The Mummy: Tomb of the Dragon Emperor*, follow.

2005
The movie *Scooby-Doo! In Where's My Mummy?* is released, in which a gang of teenage sleuths discovers the cursed tomb of Cleopatra, an Egyptian queen.

2015
In the picture book *Mummy Cat*, the pet cat of an Egyptian queen is mummified along with the queen. The cat awakens each year to see if the queen has been brought back to life.

2011
You Have to Stop This, the fifth book in the children's fantasy-adventure series The Secret Series, is published. In it, the main characters are accused of stealing a mummy from a museum.

HOW TO STOP A MUMMY

Writers of stories and movies have given monster mummies all sorts of different powers. Most have superhuman strength, but some move fast and others slowly. Mummies that were pharaohs or priests sometimes have extra powers, such as the ability to control the weather, whip up sandstorms, and even summon swarms of insects. Imagine the impossible has happened and a mummy has been brought back to life. What will you do? How will you stop it?

TRAP IT IN ITS TOMB AND RESEAL IT

You won't kill the mummy by locking it away in its tomb, but this may cause it to calm down and stay put. Remember, the mummy was probably awakened when its tomb was disturbed.

TIP: Although warnings or curses on tombs have been ignored by grave robbers and archaeologists for centuries, it wouldn't hurt to put a new warning on the door to the tomb.

UNWRAP IT

Sometimes all that is holding a mummy together is its wrappings. Try removing them, and the mummy may turn to dust.

CUT OFF ITS ARMS AND LEGS

Mummies can't fly or move around using supernatural powers. They need their arms and legs, just like you do. Cutting off the arms and legs might give you a chance to escape.

LIGHT IT ON FIRE

If a mummy cannot be stopped in any other way, it can be killed by lighting it on fire. Remember that mummies are dry, so they will burn quickly and easily. They were also prepared by rubbing the skin with oil and sealing the wrappings with resin, both of which catch fire easily.

27

THE CRYPTID RECORD

Cryptozoology's #1 Source for Sightings

Mummies Found!

Reported Sightings

While it's not likely that you're ever going to find a famous mummy up walking around, some amazing discoveries of mummies have been made. Here are some of the most well-preserved mummies that have been found outside of Egypt.

Inca Ice Maiden

The Inca Ice Maiden, also known as Mummy Juanita, is the mummy of a 14-year-old girl who lived 500 years ago. She was sacrificed in the Andes Mountains as an offering to the Inca gods and her body was preserved by the cold climate of the mountains. She was found in 1995.

Tollund Man

Tollund Man is a bog body found in Denmark in 1950. It is the mummy of a man who lived 2,000 years ago. Tollund Man was between 30 and 40 years old when he died from hanging. He was found with the rope he was hanged with still wrapped around his neck.

Otzi the Iceman

Otzi the Iceman lived between 3350 and 3105 B.C.E. in the Otztal Alps mountain range between Austria and Italy. Otzi is the oldest European mummy discovered so far. He was found frozen in ice, which preserved his body from rotting. Even the tattoos on his skin can still be seen. Otzi was found by hikers in 1991.

Lady Dai

The mummy called Lady Dai was discovered in a sealed tomb in China in 1972. Her body was wrapped in layers of silk and placed in four coffins, one inside the other. Her tomb was packed with charcoal and sealed with clay. This created a watertight and airtight resting place that preserved her body so well that her skin was still soft and she still had blood in her veins more than 2,000 years after her death.

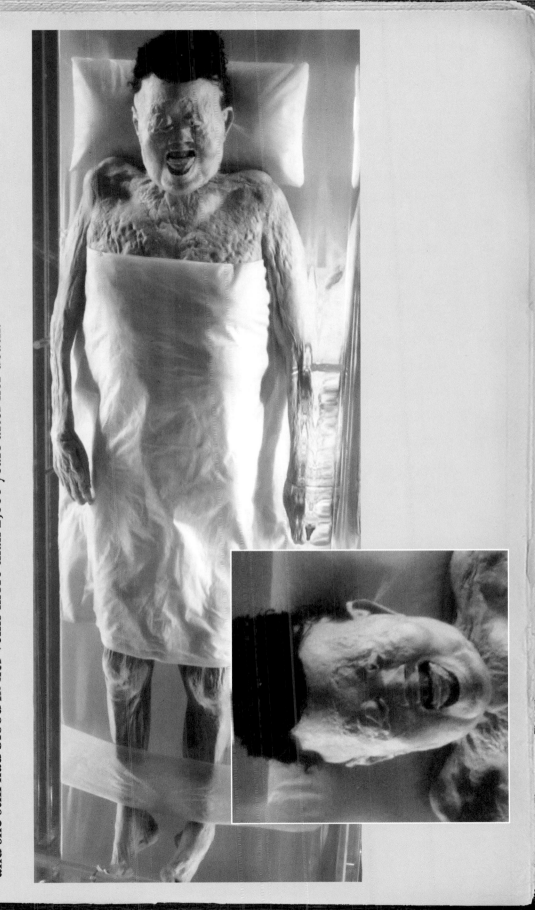

Mummies Explained

As the Christian religion spread around the world, many cultures stopped mummifying their dead. But mummification has lived on in the modern practice of embalming. Modern-day embalming involves draining the body of all of its fluids and replacing them with a chemical mixture.

Modern Mummies

Most embalmed bodies today are placed in coffins and often buried. These bodies slowly decompose. But some bodies are embalmed in ways that preserve them for even longer. World leaders Vladimir Lenin (Russia) and Mao Zedong (China) have been embalmed and placed on display so that people can see them, years after their deaths.

Celebrating the Dead

Mummies don't come back to life, but in some cultures the dead are celebrated as though they are still with us. During the Day of the Dead celebration in Mexico, people celebrate their dead ancestors by making altars at home that have their relatives photographs and favorite foods on them. They also visit and decorate family graves on this day.

Animal Mummies

Ancient Egyptians not only made human mummies, they also mummified the bodies of animals that were pets, sacred to their beliefs, or to be used as food in the afterlife. The animals below have been found mummified in Egyptian tombs.

Cats

Crocodiles

Ibises

Jackals

Baboons

LEARNING MORE

Want to know more about cryptids, myths, and monsters such as the ones described in this book? Here are some resources to check out on your cryptid-hunting quest.

Books

Mummies Exposed! by Kerrie Logan Hollihan. Abrams Books for Young Readers, 2019.

Undead Monsters: From Mummies to Monsters by Katie Marsico. Lerner Publications, 2017.

TV and Films

Monstrum is a series of videos created by PBS about monsters, myths, and legends.

Find the videos on the PBS website at:

www.pbs.org/show/monstrum/

Websites

The Centre for Fortean Zoology is a cryptozoology organization that researches cryptids from around the world. They produce a weekly TV show, books, and magazines about cryptids.

www.cfz.org.uk/

GLOSSARY

acidity The level of acid in something such as soil or water. Acid is a substance that dissolves or breaks down materials.

afterlife The belief that a person's spirit or soul lives on after death

ancestors The people in your family that came before you, from recently to long ago

ancient Egypt A civilization in northeast Africa from about 3100 B.C.E. to 332 B.C.E.

cholera A deadly bacterial disease that affects the small intestine (a digestive organ), and causes severe diarrhea, vomiting, and dehydration

curse Magical words that bring trouble or bad luck to someone

death mask A face mask made of wood, plaster, or precious metals that looks like the dead person and is placed over the face before burial

enslave To take away someone's freedom and treat them as your property

excavation The act of digging up, revealing, or removing items from an archaeological site

folklore The stories, customs, and beliefs that people of a certain place share and pass down through the generations

Indigenous peoples The first people to live in a place

inscribed Having words or markings that are written or carved

Norse A word that describes something related to Scandinavia, a part of the world that includes Norway, Denmark, and Sweden

peat A spongy material made of partly decayed plants

preserve To prevent from rotting

shapeshifting The ability to take a different form or shape

virus A type of germ that causes sickness

INDEX

CRYPTID GUIDES: CREATURES OF FOLKLORE

Could mummies be real?
This Cryptid Guide will help you decide!

TITLES IN THE SERIES:
Guide to Bigfoot
Guide to Chupacabras
Guide to Mummies
Guide to Sea Monsters
Guide to Unicorns
Guide to Vampires
Guide to Werewolves
Guide to Zombies

Teacher's Guides

Crabtree Publishing
crabtreebooks.com

GRL: U
ISBN 978-1-0396-6393-0